103 Crafts & Activities for Preschoolers &Toddlers

Year Round Fun & Educational Projects You & Your Kids Can Do Together At Home

Katherine Smiley
Copyright© 2014 by Katherine Smiley

103 Crafts & Activities for Preschoolers &Toddlers

Publisher: Enlightened Publishing

ISBN-13: 978-1499615906

ISBN-10: 1499615906

Disclaimer

The Publisher has strived to be as accurate and complete as possible in the creation of this book. While all attempts have been made to verify information provided in this publication, the Publisher assumes no responsibility for errors, omissions, or contrary interpretation of the subject matter herein. Any perceived slights of specific persons, peoples, or organizations are unintentional.

This book is not intended for use as a source of legal, business, accounting or financial advice. All readers are advised to seek services of competent professionals in the legal, business, accounting, and finance fields.

The information in this book is not intended or implied to be a substitute for professional medical advice, diagnosis or treatment. All content contained in this book is for general information purposes only. Always consult your healthcare provider before carrying on any health program.

Table of Contents

Introduction

I used to be a nanny for four children and I loved the busy schedule because it really made my workday fly by. However, one of the best parts of the day was after the chaos of the morning rush was over and the three older kids were on their way to school. Then, I could brainstorm up fun activities to do with the youngest child in the family that would keep us occupied for a while.

He was so ready to explore what the world could offer him in terms of mental stimulation and hands on learning, as are most preschoolers. It was fascinating watching how amazed and sometimes amused he became during certain craft creations and when we played games.

A lot of the activities would get him to think critically and ask relevant questions that I was only too happy to answer. It was most heartwarming to see how excited he was to present the products of our days to his parents and family when they got home.

Toddlers and preschoolers can be difficult to keep them from distracted because their attention spans tend to be short lived. Yet, they are curious and imaginative and so much fun to spend time with. Furthermore, most young children just want to be entertained throughout the hours of the day and are eager to learn anything they can.

Now, you too can collaborate with your little one on art masterpieces and decorative crafts, as well as play educational games. Whether you're a parent, nanny, day care provider, or preschool teacher, you can benefit from the long list of activities I provided in this guide to stimulate children's minds and keep their hands busy for hours.

In this guide you will find a wealth of ideas to share with your young child. Some of the activities require your close supervision as potentially dangerous supplies or tools might be involved. Many of the arts and crafts projects will result in beautiful seasonal decorations to display in your home. You will be astounded by the creations you can make with your preschooler, who will, alternatively, be enthusiastic about tapping their imagination, enhancing

4

their knowledge, and most of all, spending valuable time with you.

The Best Way to Use This Book

The activities are split into four main categories that correspond to the four seasons. Many of the projects can be done during any season, but the subcategories are themed. Thus, the first subcategory is a "Let's Go" type of category. "Let's Go Fishing" falls under Spring activities, "Let's Go on a Safari" is found under Summer, and so on.

The second subcategory of each season contains two subjects of which the first four activities can be thought of as more masculine while the last four can be thought of as more feminine (although this is not necessarily so in each case). The first example is "Pirates and Princesses" under the Spring category where the first four activities are pirate themed and the last four are medieval or princess themed.

All the other seasons have similar subcategories and all the activities are explained in thorough detail using uncomplicated supplies to make original crafts and engage in unique games.

Enjoy!

I. Spring

Let's Go Fishing

Activity #1: Reel 'Em In

Make a pole and decorate some fish, and see how many letters, numbers, shapes, and colors your little one can catch!

For a very fun fishing game, you will need a long, sturdy stick or rod, some string, and a magnet. Tie one end of the string to the end of the stick, and the other to the magnet, which acts as your bait. Then, cut out some fishy shapes from different colored construction paper or drawing paper.

Have the kids decorate the fish any way they like, but make sure that they leave space for you to add letters, numbers, or shapes. You can write the numbers and letters on with a marker, or use those extra mailbox stickers you have laying around. Either way, add a paperclip to each of the fish. This is the metal that will become attracted to the magnet.

Now, throw the fish on the carpet or floor, making sure to spread them out a bit. Have the children take turns fishing. Every time they pull up a fish, ask them if they can tell you the correct letter, number, or shape on the fish, and the correct color of the fish, too. If they are right, add that fish to his or her keep pile. If they do not know the correct answer, they must put the fish back onto the floor.

The child with the most fish at the end wins, and maybe gets to choose the next activity as a prize! Kids love this game! And it's educational, too!

Activity #2: An Aquarium To Eat

Using Blue Jello and Gummy Fish

You can make an edible aquarium that's fun for kids to eat, and yummy for adults, too! This treat can be made in either small plastic cups (for individual servings), a large punch bowl (great for a party) or in any type of clear plastic container that's suitable for food use and can be put in the refrigerator. You will have to follow the directions on the box of blue Jello to determine the amount you will need to make for whichever container you use.

Then, make the Jello, also according to the instructions printed on the box. Pour your mixture into the container and let it cool in your refrigerator for about an hour. You only want to let the Jello set partially so that you can add some swimming friends.

After that hour in the fridge, pull out your partially set Jello and add some gummy fish of different colors to your edible aquarium. You will want to push some down and leave some closer to the surface to vary the fish and make it seem like they're swimming. Put your creation back into the refrigerator and let it set completely. When it's done, you will have a fun, fishy treat to share with any little ones.

Activity #3: Betta Fish Habitat

An easy pet and a home decoration.

Most children love pets but they can be a lot of work! Betta fish are easy to take care of and can satisfy your small child's desire for a pet. Even better, you can make a betta fish habitat that serves as a piece of elegant home décor, too.

First, pick a vase. Betta fish do not need a ton of room and indeed, prefer to live in a small container. You might already have a glass vase that's the perfect size, but if not, they're easy to find. Make sure it is one that is tapered at the top. Have your little one fill the bottom with about two inches of colorful stones, marbles, or shells. Add some small aquarium decorations if desired.

Some craft stores have betta fish/plant kits that come with a vase and a piece of plastic. If you cannot find one of these kits, you will need a small piece of plastic that you can cut a hole into. The plastic is going to keep the plant from falling in, so it should fit down into the top a bit, but not fall all the way into the vase.

Plants that thrive in water can be found in nearly any hardware or garden supply center. Just make sure to read the directions or ask questions if you are not sure about a certain plant.

Finally, you and your child can go pick out a betta fish! They come in a multitude of colors so pick one that is your child's favorite color or one that matches your room's scheme. Either way, do not choose two males and put them together, or they will attempt to kill one another. Once you pick out your betta, don't forget to buy a little canister of food for it. Remember to clean the habitat about once every two weeks.

Activity #4: Jellyfish Mobile

A sting-free project!

To make a colorful jellyfish, take a paper plate and glue on different colors of paper streamers or crepe paper to the part of the plate you would normally put the food on. You can also poke different colored pipe cleaners through the plate and bend a small bit so that it will stay. In addition, different colored strings hanging down amidst the pipe cleaners and paper add another subtle touch.

Then, hold your plate so that the tentacles (pipe cleaners and paper) hang down. The plate is the top of your jellyfish. You can add eyes and decorate it any way your child wishes to. Make about four to six of these and then attach them to a coat hanger with string for a custom under the sea mobile. Make sure to hang the jellyfish at different height levels so that they are varied.

Activity #5: Sparkly Rainbow Fish

Made from common kitchen supplies.

Grab a paper plate, a coffee filter, and some tinfoil to make this shiny, bright fish. Oh, and a pair of scissors and some colorful markers, too. Spread the coffee filter (white or brown, does not matter) out flat on the plate. Color in sections with different colored markers (these can just be scribbles) until the whole filter is covered.

Then, take a spray bottle with water or your own fingers and sprinkle the filter until it gets wet enough to crinkle up some. You can either leave it to dry, or use a hair dryer on the lowest setting to blow dry the filter.

Once dry, cut out a fishy shape (with a top fin, a bottom fin, and a tail). Cut some triangle shapes out of the tinfoil and glue them on for scales. Draw an eye and a mouth on your fish and there you go! A group of these rainbow fish together look stunning, also, either on a mobile, or glued onto a sheet of paper.

Activity #6: Be Crabby

Hand and Feet prints

Every child wants to be an animal and what better way to teach them how to crab-walk than to make them become a crab first!

To do this, grab a large sheet of paper and red finger paint. Pour some paint onto a plate and have your child first dip their foot into the paint and step in the middle of the paper. Wash their foot off quickly, then have them dunk both hands into the paint and make a hand print with the fingers spread on either side and a little above the foot print. Again, wash those hands!

Now, you have to fill in the rest of your crab. Draw a head above the toes with two antennae and two eyes. Attach the handprints (the claws) to the body (the foot) with some thin, red arms. Add six little legs around the body, and your child couldn't be any crabbier! While the picture dries, chase your little one around while you both do the crab-walk for some great exercise.

Activity #7: Hands Up for School

A school of fish that is!

This creative craft is especially fun with a group of children, such as at a daycare center or preschool, but it can work just as well with a single tot or only a few kids, too.

Determine the size of paper you want for your canvas. If you want a large masterpiece or if you have a large group of children, you can choose a poster size sheet of paper or larger.

Pull out some finger-paints and plop the colors onto paper plates or plastic sauces that are big enough for a child's hand to fit in it flat. Explain to your child how they should put their hand on to the paper once it's covered in paint. No matter which hand they choose to make a print with, their thumb should be pointing to the top of the paper.

Now, have them dip their hand into one of the colors and put a print on the paper, with their thumb pointing to the top. This is the first fish. The thumb is the top fin and the fingers represent the wispy tail.

You can either have them do their fish all of the same color, or have them wipe their hand off and choose a different color to print other fish. Either way, you should end up with a monochromatic or colorful school of fish!

Not all of the fish need to be swimming the same direction, either. If the child wants to use the other hand that they hadn't used at first, those handprints can become fish that are facing the others. After you have finished all of the handprints, have your child wash his or her hands and let the paint dry.

Once the paint is dry, you will need to add some decorations to your ocean scene. With a marker, add eyes and lips to your fish. Or, you can glue on plastic craft eyes. Then, draw and color in some seaweed, coral, shells, or other underwater creatures as the background.

You can also use green crepe paper for seaweed, real shells, and sandpaper cut into the proper shapes for coral, too. Finally, you can color in the background with a blue crayon if you want, or you can fit a layer of blue tinted saran wrap over the whole picture (this works particularly well if you included any glue-on, 3-D elements).

When you're all done, admire your project for as long as you like and then it hang it in your kid's room or the bathroom to showcase your collaborative creation!

Activity #8: Goldfish Bowl

A Paper Plate Picture

For this fabulous art project, you need two paper plates. Cut out the middle of one of them while your tot draws or pastes a couple goldfish on the middle of the other one. Add some decorations to your scene, such as colored stones and a tiki head.

Now, you want to cover the hole in the one plate with either clear or blue saran wrap. Make sure you attach the wrap on the side of the plate you would normally eat on. Then, turn the plate with the middle cut out upside down and attach it to the decorated plate (so that you can see your goldfish and scene through the hole). You can attach the two plates with staples, tape, or glue.

Activity #9: Baby Turtles

You can't make just one.

When you are done with your eggs, don't throw the carton away! Well, as long as it's cardboard. The Styrofoam cartons are difficult to decorate and paint.

Take your cardboard egg carton and cut out the cups where the eggs previously sat.

These are now going to become turtle shells. Have your child or children decorate the shells with paint, markers, stickers, sequins, glitter, or just about anything they want.

While they are doing so, you can cut out some turtle feet, heads, and tails. Green foam core works the best, but these can definitely be out of construction paper or even fabric. The head should be circular, the tail should be a long triangle, and the feet can either be simple rectangles, or you can cut toes out.

Once the shells are done, glue on the other pieces of the turtle's body and glue on craft eyes or draw some on the head. Make a whole set of baby turtles; it's a great way to recycle and they're so adorable for a spring table setting, too.

Activity #10: A Whale of a Tale

The smallest and cutest whale in the whole ocean.

To make a really fun whale, take a paper bag (either a lunch size bag or a large brown grocery bag) and paint it blue for a blue whale or black and white for an orca whale. Then, stuff some crumpled up newspapers into the bag to make the body.

You want to stuff at least two thirds of the bag with newspaper. Gather the rest of the bag (where the opening is) and put a rubber band around it. Fluff out the paper beyond the rubber band and you've got a whale tail.

The bottom of the bag has become the face, so add craft eyes or draw some right onto the bag. Also add a mouth. Then, cut out some fin shapes from construction paper. Glue or tape them to the bottom of the whale, so that they stick out the sides.

Carefully poke a hole into the top of the bag a few inches from the face for the blow-hole. Take blue tissue paper, gather it together at the bottom and insert into the hole (you made need tape to secure it there). Now you've got your own ocean pal!

Pirates and Princesses

Activity #11: Jolly Roger

Ahoy mateys!

Every pirate has a unique flag to fly at the top of his or her ship. Your little pirate can have their own flag, too, with a bit of construction paper, glue or tape, and a little bit of creativity.

Use a black piece of construction paper for the background if you want it to be authentic, and choose a white sheet to cut out shapes. You can cut out a skull and crossbones, or you can make shapes that are unique and represent your child better.

For instance, if your little one likes tennis, cut out a tennis ball, or if they like pizza, cut out a slice of pizza. Then, simply glue or tape your shapes onto the background paper and you will be ready to sail to uncharted waters!

Activity #12: Buried Treasure

Finders Keepers

Here's a great way to use up some old paper bags! Take a shoebox or other small cardboard box and cover it with brown paper bag material. Draw on some leather straps and a keyhole to make it look like a treasure chest and fill it with fake gold, jewels, or other small goodies. Have your little one take a rectangular piece of the paper bag and crumple it up and rip the edges while you go hide the treasure.

When you return, flatten out the paper bag and draw a map on it with four or five landmarks (such as a piece of furniture, door, tree, etc.) with an X on the spot where you hid the treasure. See if your child can find it.

You can do this more than once and then the box and maps can be used again during a play date or other pirate pretend day.

Activity #13: Pin the Eye Patch on the Pirate

Arrrrr!

A wonderful pirate party idea, the traditional game Pin the Tail on the Donkey gets a new twist!

With Pin the Eye Patch on the Pirate, have your child or children draw the bust of a pirate on a large piece of paper. Cut out an eye patch (or more than one, maybe in different colors, for a large group of kids) from black construction paper and add a piece of Velcro on the back of it. Add the other half of the Velcro on one of the pirate's eyes. Blindfold each child on their turn to see how close they can get to the pirate's eye.

Another way to make this screamingly fun game last longer is to play Pin the Hat, Pin the Hook, or Pin the Gold Tooth on the Pirate. Any way you play, hilarity is sure to ensue!

Activity #14: Dress Like a Pirate

A custom costume!

Kids will have a great time making accessories for their pirate costume to play games with their mateys. All it takes is some common household supplies, some craftiness and creativity, and some enthusiastic children to make all you need to dress up like a pirate!

Every outfitted pirate needs a hat of course! What better hat than one made out of recycled newspaper? It's a classic!

Open up a sheet of newspaper all the way. Cut about a quarter off one side so that it will fit a young child. Fold the newspaper in half. Then, fold the outer corners down to meet in the middle about two inches from the bottom. Secure with tape. Take the top sheet of the paper at the bottom and fold it up, creasing it at the bottom of the triangles. Flip the hat and fold up the other side. Now, draw a skull and cross bones with black marker on both sides of the hat, open it up a little and place it on your child's head. Thar ye go!

In order to make a pirate hook, get a Styrofoam cup and poke a small hole through the bottom of the cup. Crumple up some tin foil and shape it into a hook. Insert the bottom of the hook into the hole in the cup and secure it there with duct tape. Cover the rest of the cup with duct tape (which comes in all colors, so you can choose to use the basic black or grey, or any other color you can find). Now you've got a pirate hook for your little one to put on his or her hand and wave around.

For a faux beard, all you need are some fluffy cotton balls, some black paint, string, scissors, and paper. Cut out a large oval from the paper. Then, cut out a skinnier oval at the top of the first one (as a whole for the mouth). Have your child paint the cotton balls black, then glue them onto the paper when it dries. Finally, glue a piece of string on either side of the beard and tie it behind the head. Now you look like Long John Silver!

Activity #15: Royal Hats

Fit for a princess.

Princess crowns and hats are a must for any royal beauty. They're also simple and fun to make!

In order to make a cone hat, take a large piece of construction paper (pink is always a good choice for princesses, but the paper can be any color). Tape a piece of string that is between 14 to 16 inches long to one corner of the construction paper. With a pencil, draw a quarter of a circle using the string as a guide. Then, cut out the quarter of a circle.

Now, glue crepe paper or long strips of scrap fabric at the corner tip to stream out from the top of the cone hat. Roll up the hat and staple/tape it together. Have your little one decorate the hat with stickers, rhinestones, drawings, glitter, etc. and there you have it! A tall, pretty hat to show off!

On important occasions, a princess needs a crown to wear. As do princes, queens, or kings. Craft foam works great for this project, and it comes in a multitude of colors.

Draw a template right onto the craft foam for your crown. If you have a large enough piece, try to make the crown big enough to wrap around your child's head. If you can't, that's fine. You can just add a piece of elastic or string to the back to fit.

Make sure either way you make the crown, you curve it a bit to match the shape of a head. All right, cut out the template from the foam while your little one gathers together faux gems, rhinestones, glitter, etc. to embellish the crown. Attach the decorations with glue, set the crown on top of your child's head and you've got one royal tot!

Activity #16: Members of the Court

Toilet paper rolls become medieval characters

Children love to play with the cardboard rolls that come with toilet paper and paper towels. It's a great idea to save the rolls in your craft room or craft box every time you are finished with your toilet paper because these little rolls are great for any number of projects. For this particular activity, you will need at least five rolls to make members of the royal court. You can make as many as you want, however.

For this, you can get as simple or as complicated as you and your child wish to. An easy way to complete this craft is to have your little one color a king, queen, prince, princess, and court jester in a medieval themed coloring book and then cut the characters out and glue them onto the toilet paper rolls.

For a more custom look, cut out different shapes from colored construction paper for different layers of your person. For example, for the king, you can cut out a strip of dark purple to attach on the bottom of the roll, then a strip of red for his cape, that you will glue above the purple, overlapping slightly. A white collar with black dots will make a nice addition.

Then, draw a head on a circle and attach that. A couple cotton balls make a wonderful beard and hair. Finally, cut out a small crown from yellow construction paper and glue it to the top.

If you want, you can add arms by poking pipe cleaners (cut to size) into the sides of the roll. Follow the same steps for the queen, prince, princess, and court jester, using your imagination for colors and designs of each of the characters.

If you are so inclined (and if your little one is still willing) you can make a fairy, an elf, some dukes and duchesses, or whatever you and your child can dream up.

Activity #17: Create a Castle

A fairy tale home or a stony fortress

This craft project can get complicated if you try to make it too big, so for a small but fun castle, gather the cardboard rolls from toilet paper and paper towels. A good number is six large paper towel rolls and six smaller toilet paper rolls. Paint all of them with silver acrylic paint, or any color of your choice. When dry, you can begin to plan your castle structure.

Warm up the hot glue gun in a place where you little one can't reach it. Stack three of the tall tubes together side-by-side and hot glue them to each other. This is the back wall of your castle.

Take two of the paper towel rolls and cut the tops of them down about two inches. Attach them in the middle of the wall of three and hot glue them together. Take the last paper towel roll and cut it down about four inches. Glue this in place in front of the two others.

You should now have a pyramid shape. Cut square shapes into the tops of all of your toilet paper tubes to make them look like turrets. Then, take your toilet paper rolls and glue them around the structure you have made. Two should go in the back, and two more on each side.

Decide what color construction paper you want to make the tower roofs. Pink or purple look great for a feminine look while black and blue are more traditional colors. Curl up six triangles of the construction paper and glue the sides together. Stick these down into the tops of the paper towel tubes and glue or staple them into place. Draw arched windows on all of the tubes and a double door on the front tube. Embellish the castle in any other way you like!

Activity #18: Princess and the Pea bed

Perfect for a royal dolly.

Use the top of a shoebox for the frame of the bed. If you want a super large one, the box top to a pair of boots works well.

Take four paper towel rolls and secure them in the four corners with staples or tape to act as posts. Have your child paint and draw designs on the rolls to make the bed look more regal. Add a half-sphere shaped piece of Styrofoam will make the rolls look more like four posts of a bed, but this step is optional.

Now, take pieces of foam batting and wrap them in many different fabrics. If you're good at sewing and your child is napping or busy for a while, consider sewing the pieces of fabric shut. If not, simply staple them together or use fabric adhesive.

Stack up your colorful mattresses in the shoe box top. Take some gauzy or lacy fabric and attach to the four posts by sticking some of the fabric down into the tops and stapling or gluing it to the rolls. Then, take some ribbon and tie each piece of fabric to each post with a nice bow.

Now for the dreaded pea! A wooden bead painted green works great for a pea. Stick this between the top of the box top and the first mattress, attaching it with a dab of glue. Now your child can play with her dolls and her very own regal bed.

Easter

Activity #19: Springtime Friends

A bunch of bunnies and a clique of chicks!

Gather up some wooden clothespins and have fun with your child painting them all white. The two clips are the bunny ears, so paint a pink inside on the front of the ears.

Glue on craft eyes just below the ears, draw on a pink nose and carefully glue on short pieces of string, twine, or thin white wire for whiskers. Don't forget to attach a cotton ball on the back for a fluffy tail. Make a whole bunch of these and set them aside for now.

Make your chicks out of the large craft fuzzy balls (they come in a number or colors so if you want yellow, you should be able to find them easily. You can also choose other springtime colors like baby blue, white, pink, and light purple).

Use the largest balls for the bodies, and smaller ones for the head. The easiest way to attach the two together is with hot glue. Have your little one hand you each piece since hot glue guns can be dangerous in inexperienced hands. Then, glue on googly craft eyes and a craft feather on each side (may need to be cut down to size).

Finally, cut out some little chick feet from orange craft foam and glue them on the bottom of your feathered friends. Again, make as many of these as you want. When your tot is done playing with them, you can arrange these on the table or around the house for some decorative Easter touches. The best thing is, you can use them every year!

Activity #20: Baker's Dozen

Textured Easter eggs.

Cut out large egg shapes from cardboard or poster board. Have your child mark off a design on the egg in pencil or crayon.

They can do horizontal or vertical stripes, big polka dots, a checkerboard pattern, or whatever type of design they want. Just make sure the design has large enough areas to fill in with bunches of tissue paper.

Speaking of which, gather a variety of colors of tissue paper, full sheets or cut into small rectangles. If you have full sheets, you will want to cut it up into small rectangular shapes. It's not difficult to cut many sheets of tissue paper at the same time.

Decide which color paper you want in each partition on the design of the egg. Add Elmer's glue to one section. Then, bunch up the strips of paper in the middle and begin pushing the middle down onto the glue.

When you have filled this area, move onto the next area. Only put down glue one section at a time so that it doesn't dry before you get to it. Fill in the whole egg and you've got a beautiful Easter project.

You can make more if you have a group of children. Have each of them make their own. A bundle of stunning eggs can be placed in a basket for a display that will make the kiddies proud.

Activity #21: A Yummy Topiary Treat

Edible and a beautiful decoration.

This project is a really fun springtime activity. You will need a small terra cotta pot, plaster, a Styrofoam ball (six inches is a good size) and a wooden dowel (about a foot long). These can all be purchased for relatively cheap at a local craft store.

Cover the hole in the bottom of the pot with duct tape and then fill it with plaster. While the plaster sets, paint your Styrofoam ball with acrylic paint in any spring color or cover it with fabric.

Poke the wooden dowel down into the still wet plaster right in the middle of the pot and then poke the other end into the Styrofoam ball. Take tooth picks and poke them through a whole bunch of those foiled wrapped chocolate ovals, then stick the other end of the tooth picks into the Styrofoam ball.

Cover the entire top of your topiary with chocolates (try not to eat too many). You can add your own custom touches such as Easter grass on the top of the plaster, a ribbon around the dowel, etc. You can also have your child paint the pot before you even get started. Either way, you will end up with a deliciously sweet little tree.

Activity #22: A Baaaatiful Centerpiece

And a wooly wonder.

Recycle an old coffee can by making a lamb centerpiece that you can also put some beautiful flowers in!

Use hot glue to attach bunches of cotton balls to the outside of the can. With the opening up, glue on craft eyes or eyes that your little one made out of craft foam. You can also add a little pink nose and some small lamb ears.

Add a lovely bunch of wildflowers that you picked with your child or bought at the store. Now you've got an instant, homemade centerpiece for your Easter dinner.

If you have a long table, you can make three or four since they're fast and so much fun to create.

Activity #23: Know Your Numbers

Counting has never been this much fun!

For this fun game, have your little ones cut out and decorate egg shapes on construction paper or poster board. These should be about the size of the child's hand.

When you have about ten or fifteen eggs per child that is participating, have them get a container they can use as a basket while you write numbers and/or letters on the back of the eggs and hide them in various easy places inside and outside the house.

When everyone is ready, send the children on a hunt for the eggs. They should gather as many as they can in their baskets and make it back to you in a designated amount of time (10 minutes or so).

Now, pull out an egg from one child's basket and ask them if they can tell you the number or letter written on the back. For every egg they correctly identify, they get to keep it. The others get to go in a separate pile.

The one with the most eggs at the end wins, but everyone will have fun learning just the same.

Activity #24: Bunny Rabbit Windsock

Welcome the blustery spring days.

Cut both the top and the bottom off of a plastic two-liter soda bottle. Paint it white with acrylic paint or cover it with white construction paper.

Draw some large eyes on the front or glue on googly craft eyes. Do the same for a cute pink nose.

Glue on small white pipe cleaners for whiskers and add a cotton ball or a bunch of cotton balls glued together to the back of the bottle for a fluffy tail.

Cut out rabbit ears from construction paper or card stock and color part of one side pink for the inside of the ear.

Attach these to the top of the bottle with hot glue or staples while your child picks out strips of brightly colored crepe to put on the other end.

Attach the strips of crepe on the bottom of the bottle with glue or staples.

Last but not least, glue each end of a long pipe cleaner to each side of the top of the bottle in order to hang it in the breezeway, on the porch, or in a window for a welcoming, seasonal sight.

Activity #25: Pretty Pinwheels

Watch them spin in the wind.

Pinwheels are classic toys that mesmerize children by spinning on those gentle blustery days of spring. It is very simple to have your child make their own pinwheel, or a whole bunch of them because they do not take that much time to make.

Take a pencil that is unsharpened and one that has a nice eraser on the end. Cut out small squares (four for each pinwheel) of construction paper and have your child decorate both sides of them with Easter pictures.

Then, fold the squares in half, pulling one corner over to the opposite corner so you end up with a triangle. It's a good idea to glue a thin piece of cardboard between the papers now as it will make the pinwheel sturdier, but it is completely up to you.

Now that you have all of your squares folded it is time to attach them to the pencil. You will need a pushpin for this part. Put one corner of a triangle against the eraser and pull the corner on the upper left down to meet it, without creasing the paper. Do this for four squares and then secure them to the pencil's eraser with a pushpin.

Test out your pinwheel by having your child blow at the paper, or take it outside on a moderately windy day. Have fun!

Activity #26: Easter Basket Treasure Hunt

Find the goodies!

One of the most fun parts of every Easter for me was the treasure hunt for my basket that my mother used to send me on. You can make a treasure hunt for your child, too, to enjoy on Easter morning.

Hide their basket in a place they normally wouldn't look the night before. In the dryer, in a cupboard, in the dry bathtub or behind the couch are all fun places that your little one can reach. Now you have to write the clues for them to follow.

Collect about eight or ten pieces of paper and number them. Now use your imagination to write simple clues for your child to follow in the morning. You should send them to many different places in the house (and outside if it's safe) to collect the next clue.

For instance, the first clue can be something such as: where does Dad go to get the things he needs when his feet are cold? The answer: the sock drawer! The next clue should be in Dad's sock drawer and might read: when you're a little hungry and just want a snack, where do you go? The pantry/snack cupboard will be where the next clue is waiting for them.

Keep writing clues like this until your last one leads to the hiding place of the Easter basket! Springtime treasures await!

II. Summer

Let's Go on a Safari

Activity #27: Dum, Dum, Here He Comes

A tiger hand drum.

Have your child decorate the back of two paper plates with tiger faces. It's fun to do two different expressions, such as a happy one and a sad one, or a growling one and a scared expression, but it's up to you (and your little one).

You can paint, color, or cut out bits of construction paper for your tiger faces. Don't forget eyes, ears, a nose and whiskers, and of course, the stripes!

Tape or glue two short pieces of yarn onto the inside of one of the plates, one on each side. On the other ends of the yarn, attach small colorful beads.

Next, attach a long round wooden dowel or balloon stick to the inside of the bottom of the same plate.

Then, put the two paper plates together so that the tiger faces are on the outside. Glue the outsides of the plates together or staple them.

If you really want a louder noisemaker, throw in some macaroni between the two plates before you close them off completely. You can also just leave it hollow.

Either way, have your kids put the stick between their flat palms and rub their hands back and forth so that the beads hit the middle of either side of the plates, drumming a jungle beat perfect for the heat of the summer.

Activity #28: Riding Down the River

A natural jungle boat for the kiddie pool!

Play the game "pick up sticks!" Collect small branches and twigs from the ground or buy them from the craft store if you do not have an area to collect them from.

You will need two longer sticks for the base of your boat (eight to twelve inches long) and enough shorter twigs to cover the tops of these sticks (these should not be that much shorter, maybe six to ten inches long). Also remember to collect a large, intact leaf to use as your sail.

Set out the shorter twigs side by side and attach them together with twine or hot glue. Then, glue on the bottom two sticks on either side of the line of twigs so that they are attached to each one.

Now, take one more stick, carefully poke the leaf onto the stick twice (at the bottom and top) and glue the bottom of this mast to one side of the raft (about two or three sticks from the end).

Now your little one can send his or her toys on a jungle adventure in the kiddie pool or just on the carpet or rug inside.

Activity #29: On the Hunt

You can't go on a safari without binoculars.

For a very simple and fast project, glue two cardboard toilet paper tubes together to create a set of fine binoculars.

Have your child decorate the tubes with construction paper, markers, paint, or jungle themed stickers.

Glue on a piece of string to either tube at one end as a strap to go around your child's neck to hold the binoculars when they're not needed.

Play safari as you scour the backyard for wild animals!

Activity #30: Reach For the Sky

A giraffe pencil holder.

To make this useful craft all you will need is a coffee can, a wooden ruler, some colorful construction paper and glue.

Cover your coffee can in yellow construction paper (or any color you want) and decorate it with brown spots to mimic a giraffe print.

Hot glue a ruler straight up the inside of the can (glue about two inches to make it sturdy).

Cover the front of the ruler with the same color of construction paper as the body and add spots.

Cut out a head from the paper, add eyes ears, and a mouth and glue this on top of the ruler.

Now you can fill the can with pencils and other art supplies for the home office, bedroom desk, or for your child to take with him or her to preschool!

Activity #31: Monkeyin' Around

Swinging by all fours plus a tail.

Nothing is more fun for your little monkey than a soft bendy monkey of his or her own.

Pipe cleaners are awesome craft tools to make some fun, fuzzy monkeys that can dangle from anywhere! You can use brown or gray pipe cleaners for a realistic look, or get more whimsical and creative and make purple, green, or orange monkeys!

Take one long pipe cleaner and bend one end up, curling the very tip just a bit, for a tail.

Add another cleaner for the two legs by winding the middle of it around the first one a few inches above the end of the tail.

Do the same thing for the arms further up.

Then, wind one pipe cleaner around the middle again and again to make a body and to secure the other pipe cleaners better.

Wind a last pipe cleaner into a ball for the head and attach it to the top.

Add google craft eyes by gluing them on.

Curl the ends of the legs and arms to hang your monkey from just about any object!

Activity #32: A Rainforest Collage

Scrapbooking for the youngsters in a unique art piece.

Do you have a bunch of old magazines lying around? Scrapbook paper? Wrapping paper? Well, now you can put these objects to good use to make a beautiful picture.

Sketch out a quick jungle or savannah scene on a piece of card stock (you choose the size). You will need some large trees, maybe a river, and lots of animals.

Have your child help you plan out the picture.

Then, cut out shapes from different patterned paper and paste them on certain parts of your picture. For instance, for the leaves of one tree, you might choose a colorful yellow and green pattern. For the bark, you may have a completely different design.

You can also use magazine pictures of trees or water to add as well. You might even find a monkey, elephant, or other animal picture in a magazine to insert in your collage.

Fill up the entire space with different pictures and patterns and then frame your masterpiece or put it on the fridge so that your child can show off their artwork.

Activity #33: Beep Beep

Here we come in a Jeep!

To go on a safari, you need some sort of transportation of course. This is when you have a great time making a custom Jeep!

Take a large cardboard box and cut it to the desired shape. You may want to cut the bottom out so that your child can run around with the Jeep over his or her shoulders (in which case, attach some straps made out of elastic or fabric) or you can just have your tot sit in it and pretend to drive around. Either way, you can use pieces of Styrofoam for a steering wheel and mirrors, bottle caps for knobs and paper plates for headlights.

You can also mount two pieces of Styrofoam to the sides of the front of the box and stretch a piece of saran wrap across to act as a windshield.

If you want to really get creative, paint the box and all of the accessories in any way you want.

When the Jeep is done (and the paint has dried) send your child on safari to find animals and strange plants. Just don't forget the binoculars!

Activity #34: Shellephants

Seashore project for a cool souvenir.

This is a perfect vacation activity and something great to do with the seashells you collect on the shore.

Glue various shells together to create a unique elephant. Glue two open shells together (the insides should face each other) for the body of your elephant.

Then, take a closed spiral shell for the head and trunk and glue it to the top of the body.

Two more open shells glued to each side of the head make perfect ears.

For legs, you can use a stack of small pebbles glued together, or small pieces of driftwood. Attach small shells for the feet.

If you can find another small spiral shell, use this for a tail.

Now you've got one fantastic souvenir of your summer vacation to the sea!

Activity #35: Hear Him Roar

The King of the wild made out of recycled materials.

A snazzy lion can be made out of a paper bag, newspaper, and glue.

Draw a lion face on one side of a paper bag. This can be a brown lunch bag for a smaller lion or a great big brown paper grocery bag for a big lion. If there is something printed on one side, simply cut the paper bag and use the plain inside to draw your face on.

Add ears made out of smaller pieces of another paper bag.

Draw eyes, a nose, a mouth, and whiskers.

Then, cut thin strips of newspaper and begin gluing them around the lion face for a very cool mane.

Paste your lion on a large sheet of paper for a custom art piece, or just hang him on the wall for all to see.

Activity #36: I Can Be a Toucan

A mask for bird wannabes.

What child has never dreamed of being a bird? Now they can actually be toucans with this simple mask project.

To make a toucan mask, cut out a shape to put over the eyes (like making sunglasses without the sides). Carefully cut out the middle of each side so that the eyes will be able to see what is going on.

Look a picture of a toucan on the Internet. They have colors around their eyes, so paint or color this part of your mask to match.

Then, use a hole punch to punch a hole in either side and slip a piece of ribbon through it, knotting it at either end.

This ribbon should be long enough to fit around your child's head when they have the mask on.

To make the beak, draw a big rounded triangle shape on orange or yellow construction paper and cut it out.

Bend the triangle and make a small crease in the middle. Add two nostril shapes down at the end and maybe some glitter along the crease for effect.

Now, attach the beak to the eye part of the mask by folding a small part of the beak under each side of the eye mask and gluing or taping in place.

Fit the mask onto your little one's head and you have your very own toucan pet.

Gnomes and Fairies

Activity #37: Mushroom House

Perfect for all the little people.

You and your child can create an adorable little mushroom house or a thriving gnome neighborhood with this simple and fun craft.

Cut a Styrofoam ball in half carefully with a knife. This will be the top of your mushroom house.

Now push some brightly colored Popsicle sticks (the large ones work best) into the flat part of the half circle. Keep going all the way around the Styrofoam piece, until the first and last Popsicle stick are touching.

Now, insert the opposite ends of the sticks into the other half of the Styrofoam that you cut, with the dome going up inside the house so that it can stand flat.

Once you have the structure done, you can begin decorating your gnome home!

Cover the domed roof with red paper and glue on white dots for a classic mushroom look. Add a doorframe with little pieces of foam and glue on a bead for a doorknob.

Add windows, some tiny pots of flowers out front, and some twigs and feathers glued to the sides of the house for a nature type setting. Be as creative as you can.

If you are still having fun with this project, make a whole gnome village.

Add more mushroom houses and use a rectangular piece of Styrofoam for the base to push all of the houses down into. Add mailboxes made out of clay or paper perched Popsicle sticks.

You can also make a little pond near one of your houses by gluing down blue foam board or using blue cellophane.

Finally, add some nature touches to your village by making fake flowers on stems and putting them up against houses and near the pond, poking feathers down into the tops of the houses and around the base, as well as sticks and twigs. You can even add stone walkways made out of little pebbles.

Enjoy making this craft and playing with it when it's all done.

Activity #38: Every Gnome Needs a Job

Make a mini terrarium.

Terrariums are great to build with your children because they will learn how to plant and care for living things that require less attention than say, a new puppy (although puppies are fun, too).

You can easily make a mini terrarium by choosing a glass or plastic container. The size is up to you but make sure you choose something that you have room for on a windowsill or a table up against the window to give your plants plenty of sunlight.

Put some pebbles in the bottom of the container to allow for proper drainage. Then, add a layer of sphagnum moss (found at a local craft or floral store).

Now it's time to add your soil. Make sure you don't just put your soil down flat, but create hills and valleys to add some depth and realism.

Miniature African violets, Swedish ivy, and Button ferns are all great choices for terrarium plants, but browse the small plant section at a local garden center to see which ones will look nice together. Do not crowd the plants together. You need to leave some place for a few decorations.

Thrift stores are great and economical places to look for teeny little knick-knacks to include in your terrarium. See if you can find things like a small cottage, an old toy pickup truck, plastic or ceramic animals, dollhouse furniture (like an outdoor table and chair set) or anything else you think will look good.

You might even be able to find a wee little gnome to include, or you can make one out of clay. Add these to your terrarium for a minia-ture display that your child can be proud of.

Activity #39: Coneheads

Simple gnome community.

At your local craft store, you are sure to find Styrofoam cones in a variety of sizes. Col-lect as many as you like and get ready to transform them into adorable little gnomes!

For about half of the cone or a little more, cover in your choice of colored construction paper, circling around the pointy tip and go-ing down. This is the hat of the gnome.

Cut out a strip for the shirt and cover the rest of the cone. Then, draw and color a head beneath the hat with a cute little face.

You can add cotton balls for hair poking out of the cap, or different colored yarn for female gnome hair. Glue some real plastic buttons on the shirt for added decoration and add two small strips of black felt beneath the cone for tiny feet.

Make a whole gnome group and send them on a trip, on a picnic, or have a family reunion!

Activity #40: Knock Knock

Who lives behind that door?

Start your child off on an imaginative journey as you make craft gnome doors and then create stories about what kind of characters live behind them.

Pick a tree outside or a cabinet or cupboard inside and begin making a front door for the 'home' that lies behind it.

You can make the door out of sticks, paper, clay, or any material you like. You can add wooden beads or small pebbles for doorknobs and make a tiny wreath to hang outside or a doorknocker. You can also add a custom Welcome mat in front of the door.

Prop up your door or doors in front of a structure to act as a house and let your tot's imagination run wild.

Ask them questions such as: Who lives here? What is their name? How old are they? What do they do for work? What is their favorite playtime activity? Who is their best friend? What do they have for a pet?

Write down your little one's answers in a memory book to read back to them when they are older for a humorous and heartwarming moment.

Activity #41: Come Fly With Me

Shimmery fairy wings make you feel magical.

To make these fun and fabulous wings, you will need to cut a length of floral wire about four feet long.

Wind the wire into a figure eight with equal circles/ovals on either side.

Now, cover the wings carefully. You can use lace, tulle, any other kind of pretty fabric, or even pantyhose cut off at the knee.

Decorate the fabric with glitter glue and let dry.

Attach arm straps using elastic or fabric to the middle of the wings, making sure they are the right size to fit over your child's shoulders. Let them flit around like a fairy with their new fashionable wings!

Activity #42: Finding Fairies

They can be so elusive!

To make some quick, easy fairies, take wooden clothespins, glue on some fabric for dresses and some yarn on top of the round part for some hair.

Add two dots for eyes and one for a mouth. Then, fashion some wing shapes out of pipe cleaners and cover these with lace or tulle and attach them to the back of the fairies. Try to do at least four in different colors to play a search for and find game.

Have each fairy be worth a different amount of points. For example, the yellow one could be worth one point, the purple one could be worth two, the red one worth three, and the blue one worth four points.

Have your child or children cover their eyes while you pick a room to hide them. Hide the fairy worth the least amount of points in an easier place, and the one worth the most in the hardest place.

Then, time your tots to see how long it takes them to find the fairies. Add up their points and see who wins that round.

You can play multiple times, making this a great play date or party game!

Activity #43: Shake It Up

Captured fairy dust.

Take a clean, glass baby food jar or glass fruit jar and use it hold your fairy dust. Add white sand, sequins, and glitter of all different colors.

You can also cut up glow sticks, but know that these will fade after a few hours.

Put the cap on the jar tightly and have your little fairy carry around their magic dust to impress their friends and use when they want something magical to happen.

Activity #44: Making Wishes Come True

The magical fairy godmother.

To be a fairy godmother, you really need three things: wings, fairy dust, and a magic wand. Read above to learn how to make fairy wings and fairy dust.

For a wand, all you need is a wooden dowel, a star cut from fabric foam, and some brightly colored ribbons.

Hot glue the foam star to the top of the dowel. Then, hot glue lengths of ribbon on the back of the star so that they dangle down the length of the rod. Decorate the star with glitter if you want.

Put the wings on your child and give him or her the fairy dust and wand.

Make up wishes that will be easy for them to make come true, such as, "I wish I had a teddy bear to hold right now" or "I wish someone would color me a beautiful picture" or "I wish someone would dance for me."

Make the game fun and encourage your child to be a fairy godmother often, performing good deeds for others.

Fourth of July

Activity #45: Boom

Fireworks are a must for the fourth.

To make a beautiful, colorful firework picture you will need a large sheet of black construction paper or poster board and a whole bunch of q-tips. You will also need some different colors of food coloring.

Fill a bunch of small bowls with water and add some food coloring drops.

Remember that you don't just have to use the colors that come in the box collections; you can also make colors of your own by mixing the colors up. You can make a purple with blue and red drops, orange with red and yellow, etc.

Cut up your q-tips into a variety of lengths and then dip them into the various bowls.

Set the dyed q-tips on a paper plate and let them dry overnight, or stick them in the microwave for five minutes to dry quickly.

Once dry, glue the q-tips onto the black paper in a circular pattern. All of the cut ends should be pointing to the middle of each firework.

You can make fireworks that have all the same color q-tips, or you can mix up the colors and make a super colorful firework.

Be creative and have a blast!

Activity #46: Uncle Sam's Famous Hat

Make one for yourself.

Take two sheets of paper and draw four red stripes on one, three on the other, and all the same size. Leave some room on the paper with three stripes on one end to overlap the sheets.

Take a white, red, or blue paper dinner plate and cut out the middle to act as the brim of the hat.

Put the striped sheets of paper in a circle and tape or glue them together.

Stick the circle paper down into the middle of the paper plate and secure with tape or glue.

Last but not least, color a long strip of paper blue with white stars. Tape or glue this hatband around the base of the circle.

You can also glue the middle part of the plate you cut out on top of the hat, but this step is optional.

Plop on your little one's head and let him or her play Uncle Sam.

Activity #47: American Eagle

A fabulous bald bird puppet.

Have your child paint the part of a paper bag (small or large) that usually makes up the bottom white. This is going to be the bald eagle's head.

You can add a couple of white craft feathers at the neck if you want for effect.

Cut out a beak from orange construction paper and glue it to the middle of the head after the paint has dried. Draw or cut and paste some eagle eyes.

Then, cut out feet from orange construction paper and paste them on the inside of the bag, sticking out.

Now, fashion two wings out of paper. Sketch the shape once, but cut it out with a second sheet of paper behind the first so that you end up with two the same size.

Color them with different shades of brown and glue on some craft feathers if you want. Attach these to either side of the bag for one glorious eagle puppet.

Activity #48: Pass the Torch

Be the Statue of Liberty!

Take a paper towel cardboard tube and cover it with tinfoil.

For the top of the torch, cut a paper or plastic cup about three inches from the bottom and set this over one end of the tube, securing it in place with tape or glue. Cover this in tin foil also and make a little 'bowl' inside of the cup (so that nothing can fall through) with the tin foil.

Crumple up some yellow and orange tissue paper to imitate a flame, and then glue this down into the tin foil in the middle of the cup. You now have a torch!

A fun game to play with this object is Pass the Torch. It's like Hot Potato only with an Independence Day twist.

Have the tots stand in a circle and pass the torch to the kid of their choice while the music plays.

Turn the music off at various points and whoever is holding the torch when the music stops is out of the game until you have one child left who is the winner!

If you just want a single statue of liberty, you can craft a crown to go with the torch.

It's easy to make out of craft foam or paper. Just draw the shape of the crown on paper or foam with a pencil and cut it out. Punch a hole on either side with a hole-punch and thread a ribbon or elastic through the holes, securing with knots and a dab of glue.

Fit it onto your child's head and hand them torch. A real live Statue of Liberty is now standing in pride before you.

Activity #49: Stars and Stripes

A mobile for the holiday.

Take a wire coat hanger and bend it into the shape of a star. It is easiest to do with this with a pair of pliers.

From each point hang a number of red, white, and blue ribbons of various widths and lengths.

Add some blue, red, and silver star stickers to the ribbons (the same star stickers that many teachers use that can be found in office or craft supply stores) to make the mobile shimmer and shine.

You can also dangle red, white, blue, and silver pipe cleaners by just curling one end around parts of the wire star.

If you want, you can also cut out the letters U, S, A, or A, M, E, R, I, C, A and glue them to parts of the ribbons in the correct order.

Finally, add one piece of ribbon to the top of the wire star, tying an end into two corners, so that you can hang it from a hook in your child's bedroom, on the porch, or in the kitchen for a Fourth of July decoration.

Activity #50: A Bouquet of American Flowers

Red, white and blue hues.

For this awesome little display piece, you need red, white, and blue tissue paper as well as yellow for the middle of the flower. You will also need a bunch of plastic straws, purchased at any grocery store near the paper plates, cups, and towels.

Cut out a small square of the yellow tissue paper and wrap it around the end of a straw, taping it to secure.

Then cut out petal shapes from the other colors of tissue paper. You can cut out teardrop shapes or heart shapes for attractive petals.

Begin securing these around the middle part of the flower on the straw, with the larger petals on the outside and the smaller ones on the inside.

Make one red flower, one white, and one blue for a small simple bouquet and tie them together with a ribbon or put them in a small vase or jar. In addition, you can make flowers with a mix of the tree colors. Creativity is key to creating!

Activity #51: Little Firecracker

A safe and patriotic way to celebrate.

Take a toilet paper tube and cover it with a drawing of an American flag. You can draw this right on the tube or on a sheet of paper and cut it out to paste around the tube.

Next, cut out a circle from cardboard or card stock that is the right size to cover one side of the tube.

Poke a hole in the middle of this circle with a sharpened pencil and then glue it on one hole of the tube.

Stick a pipe cleaner in the hole (may need to be cut some) to act as a wick to the firecracker.

Then, cut out a boom shape (a star with many points) from yellow or orange paper and stick it through the other end of the pipe cleaner.

You've now got yourself an adorable little firecracker that won't be dangerous for the preschoolers in your life.

Activity #52: United States Doorway

A hanger celebrating the good old USA.

Here's a fantastic way to show your patriotism to the outside world! Have your little one help you make an all American door hanger with these easy steps.

First, you need two pieces of ribbon (red, white, or blue preferably) each two feet long. Tie them in a nice bow at the top with long strips to dangle.

Now, cut out the letters U S A from red white or blue (or a mix) paper.

Glue these on the pieces of ribbon so that they read down.

You can also add a large star on the top or bottom if you have room.

Hang this decoration on the front door to show your independent spirit.

III. Fall

Let's Be Detectives

Activity #53: I Spy

To see is not always to observe.

This classic game can be played anywhere, especially when your little one is impatient about waiting for something or someone and needs a fun distraction.

You start the game by saying, "I spy something with my little eye that is.....pink (or whatever color the object you spy is)." Now it is up to your child to guess what the object is.

You might need to give hints if they don't get it after a few minutes and begin to get frustrated.

When they have guessed the correct object, it is then their turn to 'spy' an object and have you guess.

If it seems obvious what their object is at first, guess other objects first to make their round stretch a little longer before you guess the correct object.

You can play multiple rounds of this game, outside, inside, in a parked car, at a slow event, or anywhere you need to!

Activity #54: Disguise Me

Be conspicuous as you spy.

Every good detective needs a disguise, and what is a better disguise than the old eye-glasses/mustache mask? It's also easy to make and fun to wear.

You will need a couple sheets of black construction paper, one sheet or orange, glue and scissors for this project.

Sketch out some eyeglasses on the black paper and cut them out carefully, including the center where the lens would normally go.

Then, sketch and cut out a nose from the orange paper.

Glue the nose onto the glasses in the middle.

Finally, sketch and cut out a black mustache and glue it to the bottom of the nose.

Put it on your little spy's face and they have one great disguise.

For another fun disguising project, you can make the old, "I'm just reading the newspaper, don't mind me" trick.

Take an old newspaper (maybe two or three sheets thick so make it less flimsy) and cut out two eyeholes from the middle.

Have your little one pretend to sit and read while they are really watching you carefully,

If you want, have them report two or three things you did while they watched to see how good of a detective or spy there were.

Activity #55: Fingerprint Clues

What can you make out of your fingerprints?

This fun, simple art project is also educational. Even very young children can understand that their fingerprints are wholly unique and there is not anyone else with the same fingerprint as them. Therefore, explain how police and detectives use fingerprints sometimes to find out who committed a crime.

Your child can make his or her own fingerprint drawing or a whole slew of sketches. Begin by choosing a safe non-toxic inkpad and having your little one dip his or her thumb into it and then making a print on the paper.

Wipe off their thumb and ten tell them to make a drawing around their print.

One idea is to make a flower with a stem and leaves. They could also make a giraffe by adding a long neck, head, and legs.

After the first drawing, you can have your tot make numerous prints using other fingers.

Maybe two prints become the ears of a dog or elephant. Six prints in a row can become pumpkins on a vine, a perfect drawing for the autumn season.

You can also make a large tree and put fingerprints all over the branches and some on the ground to resemble fruit like oranges and apples.

Make sure you clean up well when he or she is all done and display their pictures on the fridge, in their room, or framed and on the wall.

Activity #56: What's Been Stolen

Something to play anywhere!

Gather together about ten small objects. You might want to include little toys, erasers, smooth pebbles, or objects like these. Set them all out on a tray or a tabletop.

To start the first time, you may only put out five objects, and then a few more the next round if that is too easy, etc.

Let's see if your little sleuth has good observational skills. Tell them to look at the objects and try to memorize what they all are.

Then, have them close their eyes while you choose an object to take away.

When they open their eyes, tell them to guess what has been stolen and is missing from the group!

You can play multiple rounds of this game, and with a group of children for some extra fun.

Activity #57: Mystery Painting

What's in the picture?

See if your child's sibling or friend can guess what they drew in their picture!

Take some light colored wax crayons (white, yellow, or light pink), a piece of cardstock (preferably in the same color as the crayon you chose to make the first part of the drawing really invisible). Have your little one draw a picture with the crayon on the paper.

Now is the time to put down newspaper or wax paper on the table, counter, or surface you are going to paint the picture on.

Then, take a dark color of poster paint, put some of it in a bowl and thin it out with water.

Run a wide paintbrush coated with the thinned paint over the picture, starting from the top and working your way down.

The wax crayon lines will begin to reveal themselves. See who can guess what the picture is of first.

Activity #58: Explore Outside

A terrific twist on the scavenger hunt.

Your little detective needs something to investigate! Take him or her outside and explore nature, learning what objects come from where and who made what tracks.

Have them look at fallen apples and leaves and ask them if they can find the tree from which they fell. Investigate the ground and see if you can see any tracks (either your own or an animals). Ask them who or what made the tracks based upon the size and shape.

You might need to give them hints if it's a strange animal track like a raccoon or a deer.

Now look around for any toys or balls that have been missing for a while. Maybe one rolled under the porch or into the brush.

Carefully retrieve it and ask your child who might have lost it.

There are so many opportunities to investigate outside that you could be out all day! If so, just remember sunscreen or a large hat, even in the fall months.

Activity #59: Show Some ID

Badges for policemen and private eyes.

To make a detective badge, cut out two triangles from construction paper. Put one on top of the other upside down and glue or tape them together. Write Sheriff and then your child's name after for a sheriff badge.

For a more private eye look, cut out an oval shape and then a heart shape. Put the heart behind the oval and glue or tape them together. Now you can write Private Investigator or Private Detective and your child's name.

If you want, you can hot glue a safety pin onto the back of any badges to pin them onto your little one's shirt. Just be careful that they don't injure themselves on the sharp point of the pin.

Activity #60: Guess What Is In the Box

Solve the mystery.

This is a very simple activity but it is so much fun and can teach your preschooler about the names of different textures.

Take a shoebox and cut out a circle on one side of the box that is large enough for a hand to go through. Then, secure the box top tightly with glue or tape.

Have your child insert an object of their choice into the box (something that you don't know what it is).

Demonstrate how to reach in, feel the object and start guessing what it might be.

After you have gotten the correct answer, it's your turn to choose an object and have your tot guess what it is.

Try to choose objects that feel very different from each other, like a feather then a rock then a sponge.

Activity #61: Can You See Me Now

Magnifying glasses for little sleuths.

Take a small plastic Ziploc bag and fill it with a small amount of water (about 10% of the bag should be water).

Seal the bag tightly and then take apart a small embroidery hoop (available at any craft store).

Hold all four corners of the bag and lay it down so that the water is in the center inside one of the hoops.

Attach the other hoop so that the plastic bag is in the middle. Pull the bag tight so that it is not flimsy, then trim off the excess around the hoops.

Seal the bag with hot glue (just dab some around the hoop) and then glue a wooden dowel on for a handle.

Now your child has their very own magnifying glass for some super sleuthing!

They can look at newspapers, maps, and other small prints as well as flowers, harmless insects, and the details in small rocks. I'm sure they'll have even more great ideas to investigate.

Activity #62: Puzzle It Out

Make a puzzle that can be solved again and again.

Have your child make a colorful drawing. This can be of anything they wish, but if you need some ideas, they can draw a fall scene with pumpkins, scarecrows, and corn, or an ocean scene with various water wildlife, or even a just a farm scene with a big house and barn.

The picture could also be a holiday theme picture. Make sure the drawing is quite large (a standard size poster board drawing is fine) and make sure there are many blocks of colors within the drawing.

If your child made the drawing on flimsy paper, glue it on top of a sheet of cardboard. If the drawing was made on cardstock or poster board, it should be okay for the next step.

Carefully draw traditional jigsaw puzzle shapes in pencil on the back of the drawing and cut out the shapes.

For very young children, you want to use large shapes and maybe only six pieces for the whole picture.

When all of the pieces are cut out, shuffle them on top of a hard surface such as a table, counter top, or hard floor. Have your child attempt to put the puzzle back together.

Teach them how to look for pieces with straight edges and how to connect pieces with similar colors on them.

Another fun activity is to have two children (either siblings or friends) make pictures that you cut into pieces and then swap the pictures so that each child is doing the other's puzzle. See if the children can guess what the picture is as they put it together.

Cowboys and Native Americans

Activity #63: Wild West Costume

A hat and chaps for cowboys and cowgirls.

To make a simple cowboy hat, take a large piece of craft foam and cut out an oval. Then, carefully cut out a shape from the middle that has two bumps like a heart at the top, but keep it connected on one side of the hat (this will be come the front).

To make the flap stand up a little more, you can crease it with your hands and then add some tape to the back of the flap and the oval brim.

Cut out a band to put around the hat from paper or another color of foam. Make it look like a belt buckle in the front with a hollow square of tin foil.

Attach this to the flap. Fit the hat on your little one's head for a Wild West topper.

Now, cut a paper bag so that it opens up totally flat. Wrap part of it around the leg of your child and trim off the excess of the bag. Wrap this around the other leg and do the same.

While holding the strips around the child's legs, have them tape the sides together so they will stay put.

Draw some stripes or some cows spots on the chaps. Put on shoes that can be seen under the chaps.

Then, let your little one wear their hat and chaps with western pride.

Activity #64: Neigh Away

One footprint horse coming right up.

Do you want a keepsake from when your little cowboy or cowgirl is this small (because of course, they will not stay this way forever).

Have them make a horse picture out of a footprint to compare their preschooler feet to their adult feet when they're older.

After dipping a clean foot into craft paint, have your tot step onto a piece of paper, at a slight angle with their toes pointing to the corner. This is the head and snout of the horse.

Paint a neck with the same color paint and then draw on two eyes and two nostrils. Add ears near the top of the foot.

You can now add a mane by gluing on yarn or sponging on some darker paint between the ears and down the neck. If you want to add a halter and reins, you can do so with yarn and glue.

When all of the paint is dry, either frame this picture to hang up or keep it safe with other pieces of your child's artwork to bring out in a few years to look at again.

Activity #65: Across the West

Make a covered wagon!

To send your child's toys across the country to explore the Wild West, you will need a covered wagon. It's very fun and easy to make. All you need is the bottom of a shoebox covered with brown construction paper.

Cut out four tan wheels and draw spokes on them, then glue them to the sides of the box.

Take some pipe cleaners and make arches with them to attach to each side of the box on the inside (hot glue works best for this step).

Dab some glue on parts of the pipe cleaners and then curve a white piece of construction paper around them and hold it still until the glue sets. Also tape or glue the white paper to the shoebox.

You can attach any type of accessories to the wagon that you want.

You can put little barrels (made from toilet paper tubes with brown paper) inside the wagon or one attached to the back. You can cut out a frying pan shape and glue it on the side as if it were hanging down.

Another idea is to take a tissue and put a few crumple up tissues in the middle and close it with a rubber band for a sack of flour or sugar. Put this inside the wagon or glued to the outside as well.

When you are done and all of the glue has dried, send your covered wagon on its way to explore.

Activity #66: Desert Scene

Fun to make and delicious to eat.

Take some cucumbers and cut them into various heights, but all of them should have a flat bottom.

Glue these down onto a paper plate so that they look like cactuses (maybe one with three parts together, a lone one, etc.).

This part is optional because the pointy ends of toothpicks can be a bit sharp, but if your child is old enough or coordinated enough, you can stick toothpicks into the standing cactuses to make them pricklier.

Now thin some craft glue with water. Paint the whole surface of the plate with the glue around the cactuses and then cover it with a layer of brown sugar.

Let it dry for a bit then brush off the excess sugar that did not stick.

Add some black string licorice cut to size for some snakes in the desert.

This project is a great centerpiece for a Wild West party.

Activity #67: Dream catcher, Come Rescue Me

Expel those scary dreams.

Cut out the middle of a paper plate. Then, using a hole-punch, punch holes about three or four inches apart around the hoop of the plate you have left (closer to the inside circle) and punch three holes in the bottom of the plate.

Take some colorful yarn and have your child help you thread the yarn through the holes in the middle of the plate. Thread the yarn in a random pattern, crossing over each other.

When you are about halfway done with all of the holes, insert a bead on the yarn, then another when you're nearly done with all of the holes.

After you have threaded the yarn through all of the holes, tie off the end.

Now cut three pieces of yarn to tie into the bottom holes to hang down. Thread a few beads on each piece of yarn and then dab some glue into the center of a bead to secure a feather there.

Finally, punch two more holes close together in the top of the plate and tie a small string there so you can hang the project.

You will end up with a beautiful dream catcher that will expel bad dreams once it's hung over the bed.

Activity #68: Tiger Lily's Jewelry

Look like a Native American princess.

To make a beautiful necklace and bracelet, take a piece of yarn and thread it with large beads. You should choose wooden beads that are plain in color, with a mix of red, green, and yellow for a true Native American look, but any colors will work.

When you have strung enough beads on the bracelet, tie a knot at the end of the yarn.

Put a small dab of hot glue or craft glue inside a couple of the beads and insert craft feathers there.

For the necklace, make a longer piece, while a shorter piece suffices for a bracelet. Tie them onto your little one to play pretend Native American.

Activity #69: Tepee Toys

A wonderful Thanksgiving centerpiece.

To make these delightful little tepees that young ones can play with and you can decorate for the holidays with, take a piece of tan craft foam and roll into the shape of a cone. Secure it with hot glue then have your child draw designs on the outside with black, red, and yellow markers.

Gather up a few twigs to slide into the middle of the tepee.

Cut the tip of the cone at a diagonal angle, making the opening just large enough to insert three small twigs.

Secure the twigs with hot glue and you've just crafted your very own Native American abode!

Use in games or make a few of these and set them in the middle of your table for Thanksgiving dinner.

Activity #70: Totem Pole Beauties

Art that stands tall.

Save the tube from inside of a paper towel roll and use it to make a grand totem pole.

Cut strips of construction paper and draw animal faces on the front of them, then wrap the pictures around the tube and secure with glue.

When the whole tube is covered, you can cut out wings from cardboard and glue them to the sides of the totem wherever there is a bird face.

Stand up the totem for decoration and or let your little one play Native American games with it.

Halloween

Activity #71: Spooks in the Night

A picture of glowing eyes.

Making this art piece is super easy and fun as well!

Cut a foam board to your desired size and paint one side of it with two coats of chalkboard paint (available in any hardware store).

Using white chalk, draw a spooky forest scene, with twisted trees. Then, take a string of white Christmas lights and insert two of the tips next to each through the back of the board.

On the front of your picture, these light tips should look just like glowing eyes.

Add a few more sets of glowing eyes through the back of your board and then mount your picture on top of a mantle or table, so that the rest of the lights are hidden in the back but still provide a backlight glow to enhance the spookiness.

Activity #72: Trick or Treat

Flying bat bags to hold goodies.

Take a clean, empty milk carton and cut off the top (so that there is only the square part left). Cover all sides with black construction paper, gluing it into place.

Now cut out eyes and a mouth with two little fangs and glue on the front for the face.

Cut out bat wings from black construction paper.

You can either trace your little one's hands and cut out the shapes or sketch a more traditional bat wing (one long arch on top and three arched points on the bottom). No matter what you choose, glue the wings to the back so they stick out the sides.

Finally, attach a long strip of cardboard to the inside of the milk carton for a handle.

Carry this around to collect all of your Halloween treats!

Activity #73: Frank the Giant

Stuff the monster Frankenstein and scare your pals.

You can make a huge Frankenstein head by following these easy steps.

Open up two pages of newspaper and lay them flat down, one on top of the other.

Attach three sides with staples, glue, or tape.

Now stuff a bunch of other crumpled newspapers down into the open part.

Seal off the opening once the head is nice and full.

Here's the messy part, so you might want to do this in the garage or on top of more newspapers.

Paint the entire thing green except for the very top, which you want to paint black for the hair.

Cut out some eyes from white construction paper and glue them on the front below the hair.

Draw or paint on a mouth and nose.

Cut out ears and two screws to go on either side of the temple.

Attach these to your monster head, carry him around and listen to the giddy screams!

Activity #74: Moving Spirits

Great flapping ghosts!

Take a paper plate and draw a spooky face on the back of it with marker.

Then, attach some long strips of white crepe paper so that they hang down below the face of the ghost.

Glue these onto the side of the plate you would normally eat on.

Last but not least, glue or staple on a piece of string or twine at the top so you can hang the ghost up to frighten Halloween guests.

Activity #75: Propped In the Field

A wooden spoon scarecrow.

Gather a bunch of straw and get ready to make a fabulous scarecrow for Halloween!

Take a wooden spoon and cover the head of it with a piece of tan cloth. While it is flat on the bulbous part of the spoon, draw a quick scarecrow face.

Then, stuff some small bits of straw into the head so that they stick out of the neck a bit and secure the fabric with a rubber band around the base of the spoon.

Next, glue a Popsicle stick horizontally across the spoon, a couple inches below the neck to represent arms.

Cut a hole in another rectangular piece of cloth and pull it over the head of the scarecrow.

Gather it at the bottom of the wooden spoon and wrap it with another rubber band.

To prop him up, insert the bottom of the scarecrow into a square piece of green craft foam and you and your child can be proud of the decoration you made.

Activity #76: Creepy Crawlies

Spiders stuck in webs.

Gather together some Styrofoam craft balls of various sizes. Paint them black or cover them with black construction paper.

Glue two craft eyes on each spider and then get ready to add eight legs.

Cut black pipe cleaners to the proper sizes for your spiders and begin sticking the hair legs into the sides of the balls (four on each side).

Now string up some fake webbing (purchased at any department or Halloween store at the right time of year) where you want to show off your spiders.

Put your spiders in the webbing, attaching them by curling the pipe cleaner legs if necessary.

The end result is one creepy web display.

Activity #77: Pumpkin Patch Project

Ripe off the vine.

Use a full sheet of light green felt for the base of your pumpkin patch. You might want to glue this on top of a piece of cardboard or card stock to make the structure sturdier, but you don't have to.

Now take some brown and green pipe cleaners and fashion some vines. Make some long and skinny, make some curled around others and some sticking out in curlicues like real vines.

When you have your vines like you want them, glue them down on the green felt.

Add leaves cut out of darker green felt and glue them down.

Next, just add orange pom poms for pumpkins. Space them evenly along the vines and glue them onto the project.

You can add craft eyes to each pumpkin if you want, but you don't have to.

Make your pumpkin patch as full as you want and set it out for play and display.

Activity #78: Cackling Cup and Cone

A witcheriffic craft.

To make this fiendish female, you will need a paper cup and a Styrofoam cone.

Turn the cup upside down and glue the flat part of the cone on the underside of the cup. Do not worry if there is an overlap.

Now, cut a strip of green paper and attach it around the base of the cone. This is the witch's face so you will want to draw on eyes, a warty nose, and a mouth.

Cover the rest of the cone (her hat) with purple or black paper.

Cut out a little square with the middle cut out to glue on the hat for a belt.

For the witch's dress, cover the cup with black or purple paper and glue it to the cup.

Add a colorful belt and attach it on to the dress.

Then, cut out long thin strips of white paper and draw red stripes on them for stockings.

Glue these under the cup so they look like they are poking out of the dress. You can have them come out flat so it seems as if the witch is sitting down.

Finally, add some black shoes and your witchy gal is all done!

IV. Winter

Let's Make Music

Activity #79: Rain, Rain, Come My Way

Gentle sounding rainsticks.

Noisemakers are all the rage with youngsters, and even if they can be annoying sometimes, it's important to introduce music of all
types into your children's lives.

Take two paper towel tubes and cover up
one end of each of them with tin foil. You can
use hard, dry rice, corn, or pasta (or a mixture
of all three) to put inside the tubes.

Fill them up about a quarter of the way
and then put tin foil on the other end of the
tubes.

Now, you and your child can decorate the
tubes any way you like. You can draw directly
on them with markers or you can paint the entire tubes with fun designs and let it dry.

Show your child how to shake the rain sticks to make a rhythm and then let your little one go wild trying to make it rain.

Activity #80: Little Drummer Boy and Girl

Bada boom bada boom.

What young child does not love to bang on things? Well, now you can make a homemade drum with them to bang on so that they do not hit valuables with sticks.

Take two clean, empty oatmeal cartons (round cylinders). Cover the outside of them with paper and draw designs on the paper to make them fun and interesting.

Add two strings of elastic or large rubber bands. Then, use two wooden dowels as drumsticks.

You can also glue on a long strip of fabric to put around your child's neck to hold the drum in place as they march around and beat their new drum.

Activity #81: Chime Time

Make a sweet sounding chime set sure to delight kids.

Take a wooden yardstick, some string, and some washers of different sizes. You can find a variety of washers at any hardware or home improvement store.

Hang the washers at varying lengths from the yardstick.

After you wrap the string around the yard-stick, tie a knot and then add a dab of glue to make it secure.

String up the washers down the whole length of the yardstick.

Hang your yardstick from the ceiling (so the washers are lower enough for your child to reach) with another length of string.

Now, take some wooden spoons and show your little one how to strike the washers and run the spoons down the length so that the washers chime together.

Activity #82: Bloomin' Bagpipes

Blow into these tubes for a unique sound.

Scottish bagpipes are such strange instruments that your child may never have seen any.

Do a quick Internet search to show your little ones what bagpipes look like and play a few audio clips so they understand the sound and how they are played. Then, prepare to make your own set of gorgeous bagpipes!

Take five cardboard paper towel tubes and have your child or children decorate them with construction paper and markers. Also have them decorate a paper bag the same way.

Lay the paper bag down flat and cut four holes into the top (large enough to put the tubes into.

Put the tubes into the holes, gluing or taping them to secure them. They should be sticking out at slightly different angles, but in one row.

Using the true opening of the bag, stuff it with crumpled up newspaper so that it billows out as if it is filled with air.

Cut the last of the tubes to be a little shorter than the others and insert it into the opening of the bag, securing it in place with a rubber band.

Now wrap a couple pieces of yarn around the tall tubes for effect.

Hand it off to your little musician and let them hum into the tubes as much as they want.

Activity #83: Strumming Along

A banjo to help learn shapes.

Your child can now learn the names of shapes by making this cool banjo to play!

It's nice to do this project with different colored construction paper so that young children do not get confused, but that's up to you.

First, cut out a large circle from one color of construction paper and a smaller circle from another color. Then, cut out a long rectangle (the neck of the banjo) from another.

Cut out a small square from yet another color and finally, four little triangles from the last color of construction paper.

Set your shapes on a piece of cardboard in a banjo and trace them. The small circle should be on top of the large one; the long rectangle is the neck of the banjo with the square at the other end and the little triangles coming off the sides of the square (two on each side).

Once you have traced the banjo onto the cardboard, cut it out while your child practices the names of the shapes.

Then, have him or her help you glue the shapes onto the correct places; naming what each shape is as they do so.

Make sure all of the edges of the paper are glued down securely.

Last but not least, take two long pipe cleaners and carefully poke one side of each into the top square, folding them over in the back and gluing or taping them down. Then poke the other end into the small circle and do the same to attach.

You can also use elastic or rubber bands for the strings (these will actually make a noise) but know that they can be a bit dangerous for little fingers.

Activity #84: Shake, Rattle, and Roll

Fun, homemade maracas.

Take two empty water bottles and wrap them in each masking tape or duct tape.

They make duct tape that comes in all different patterns and colors, so you could cut strips from different kinds and make a design as you wrap the bottle. Or, you could just use masking tape and then draw a design with markers.

When you're done making your bottles look awesome, fill them with dried beans or rice, or popcorn kernels.

You want to fill up the bottles about half way. Screw the cap back on tightly (you might also want to tape this up just in case) and then start shaking your new maracas.

For a surprise to other family members, you might want to help your little one come up with a short routine to perform after dinner as entertainment.

Activity #85: Magnificent Mouth Instruments

A kazoo, a horn, and a flute.

Kids love to put things in their mouths, which can sometimes be very dangerous, but now they can help make their own instruments that use the mouth. These will be safe and fun at the same time.

The first instrument to make is a simple kazoo.

Take a plastic comb and make sure it is very clean. Then, put a piece of tissue paper over the teeth of the comb and glue it to the solid part of the comb on the top and bottom.

Have your child put the part with the paper over the teeth between their lips and begin humming. Instant kazoo!

Next, you and your little one can make an easy but cool horn.

Take either a toilet paper tube or a paper towel tube (the desired length is up to you or up to what is available).

Cut a small piece of wax paper and put it over one end of the tube, making it secure with a rubber band. Then, decorate the horn with markers, paint or stickers.

Blow into the other end like you would a real trumpet and have a noisy blast!

Flutes in a variety of forms have been around since ancient times because they are small and easy to carry, and they also make appealing sounds.

To make your very own flute, cut a cardboard tube from a roll of wrapping paper (generally a little thinner than paper towel tubes) to the right size (about a foot long is good).

Carefully poke some holes into the tube. You want a larger oval hole to blow in at one end of the tube.

Then, you need some holes that will be easily covered with fingers down the length of the tube. Anywhere between three to six holes will work.

Now you can decorate your flute with markers, colored tape or paper, or glitter. Let your child be creative with this step.

Tie a piece of a yarn with a bead on it around the end of the flute for an added touch.

Hold the flute up horizontally and blow into the large hole, using your fingers to cover holes at random to make various sounds. See if you can pick out a tune!

Activity #86: Zany Xylophone

A whole tin set to wail away on.

To make an easy xylophone that's a big hit with the tots, you will need to gather together a bunch of empty tin cans. These can be paint cans, coffee cans, canned vegetable cans, etc.

Make sure they are all sparkling clean before making your xylophone.

You can use rubber bands to attach the cans, but very young children like to play these and sometimes snap them on their fingers for a striking boo boo.

Masking or duct tape might be a better option, especially for the real little ones.

Okay, decide on the layout you want your xylophone to be in. The largest can might go in the middle of the bunch.

Once you have arranged the cans, attach two together with a rubber band or tape. Then, attach a third can to those two and keep going until all of the cans are in a bunch.

If you use masking tape, it might be fun to decorate it with stickers or marker designs.

Grab a few unsharpened pencils for mallets, or use toy mallets (available in many toy stores).

Demonstrate how to strike different cans for different sounds.

Let your little one become one rocking xylophone player.

Activity #87: Jingle Bells

A tinkling tambourine project.

Attach two paper plates together by setting one upside down on the other (so that both sides where you eat are facing each other.

Glue or tape them and then decorate them with paint, markers, crayons, or stickers.

Punch holes all the way around the edges of the plates, about two or three inches apart.

Now tie a bell (available at many craft stores) in each hole with string or yarn. Make sure you knot them tightly before handing the instrument off to a child so that the bells do not go flying as they begin to shake and hit the tambourine.

Listen to the joyous sound of the bells as you prepare to decorate for the winter holidays.

Activity #88: Five Pipers Piping

Panpipes that teach about measurement.

To make a set of panpipes, you will need five cardboard paper towel tubes (there are so many cool things you can make with these tubes).

Line up the paper towel tubes side by side. Cut each paper towel tube about an inch shorter than the one preceding it so that the sizes end up in descending order.

Now, take duct tape and wrap it around all of the tubes, making sure they keep staying in a straight line.

You might want to wrap the duct tape more than once to get a secure instrument.

Decorate your tubes with markers or stickers and have your little one show off his or her piping skills by demonstrating how to blow over the top of the tube (just like blowing into a soda bottle).

For an advanced set of panpipes that make a more realistic sound, cut tubes from half-inch PVC piping, again with one about an inch shorter than the one that comes before it.

Use duct tape to hold them together as well. Duct tape a penny on the bottom of each tube.

This set is one you might need to do while your preschooler naps and surprise them when they wake up with a new musical toy.

Snowmen and Penguins

Activity #89: Step On It

A footprint snowman.

Snowmen are such wonderful beings and they can be made in so many other ways than just outside in the snow (although these are fun to make as well).

You can make an easy snowman with your child's footprint by having him or her dip a foot into white craft paint and stepping onto a sheet of black or dark blue construction paper.

Let the paint dry while you wipe off the foot and then cut out a top hat from another color of construction paper to glue on the heel of the foot (the toes will be the bottom of the snowman).

Add some eyes and a pointy nose, then glue on some small twigs on either side of the foot for arms. Add a scarf by painting or drawing with marker or by pasting a bit of fabric on your picture.

You might always want to paint some white snow beneath the snowman or around it as if the snow is falling.

Activity #90: Squishy Snowpeople

Yummy and great to make.

These wonderfully delicious goodies are sure to tantalize the taste buds of anybody who tries them. They are very fun to make and are excellent ideas for winter or Christmas themed parties, especially for the little ones in your life.

Have your child help you stack three large marshmallows onto a lollipop stick by poking the stick through each in turn. Then, take a thin chocolate wafer and spread a bit of peanut butter on top.

Stick a peanut butter cup on top it and then slide both onto the stick to be the hat of the snowman. Add candy buttons and eyes and a fruit roll up scarf.

Finally, stick pretzel sticks into the middle marshmallow for arms.

Make a bunch of these for adorable and yummy treats.

Activity #91: A Smiling Snow Family

To represent your own!

Have your child make a snow family that resembles his or her own family.

For the adult snow people, glue to Styrofoam or paper cups together, the top one upside down so that the rims are glued together. For the children in the family, just turn a cup upside down and they will be the perfect size.

Cut some small squares out of colored construction paper and shape them into a cone to glue on the top for winter hats.

Glue on a small pom pom as well if you want. Then, draw some eyes and stick a cut orange pipe cleaner into the cups to make noses.

Finally, glue on some buttons and you've got yourself an adorable little snow family.

Activity #92: Hang 'Em Up

Light but fun ornaments for the tree.

Gather some Styrofoam balls in various sizes so you can make small, medium, and large snowmen.

Have your child help you glue them together in groups of two or three. Then, use a
Sharpie marker to draw some eyes and a nose
on the head of your snowmen.

Wrap a piece of colorful fabric around
them for scarves.

Glue on some small buttons and then a
string at the top so that you and your child
can hang your creations on the Christmas tree.

Activity #93: Bottle Tottle

An adorable penguin.

Take an empty plastic two-liter soda/juice
bottle and carefully cut a small flap in one
side.

Put a ball of clay about the size of your first
into the bottom to keep the bottle from tipping
over. Then tape the flap shut. Now take a
white athletic sock and pull it over the bottle,
starting from the bottom.

Pull it tight and hook a rubber band
around the sock and bottle top (with the cap
off). Use a pencil or the handle of a wooden
spoon to squish the rest of the top of the sock
down into the bottle. Either glue the cap back
on with hot glue or use the cap to a bottle of
laundry detergent (this cap is more hat-like).

Now it's time to decorate the penguin!

Cut out some black wings and some orange feet from craft foam. Glue the wings on either side and the feet on the bottom. Draw or cut and paste eyes and a beak.

Finally, add some buttons, a bow tie, or a long scarf. Make a buddy for your first penguin so that you and your child can play pretend with them!

When you're done, you can keep these fine friends as winter decorations.

Activity #94: Penguin Puppet Show at Noon

Fantastic finger puppets.

It's incredibly easy to make cute penguin finger puppets.

Cut out rectangles from black construction paper and wrap them (a little loosely but still snug) around your child's finger then tape it to secure.

Have your child put one finger down on white construction paper and trace around the finger. Cut these out and paste them onto the black body for the penguins' stomachs.

Glue on craft eyes and a small orange paper triangle for a beak.

Make enough penguins for your children and their friends to put on a spectacular puppet show!

Activity #95: Shivery Friends

The c-c-c-cold but cool penguins.

Cut out a large oval shape from cardstock or cardboard for each penguin you are going to make.

Sketch out an oval in the middle and a triangle above for a beak. Collect a bunch of squares of black, white, and orange tissue paper (either pre-cut or cut the squares from full sheets of paper).

Crumple up the squares with your child and glue them on to your penguin one by one. You want to use black for the body and head of the penguin, white for the middle oval, and orange for the beak. Crumple up a few white ones for the eyes as well.

To make this craft go faster (since young children can be impatient sometimes) put down a bunch of glue and then see how many tissue paper squares you can crumple and put down as fast as you can.

If you want to add some personalized touches, you can put earmuffs on either side of the head and a pipe cleaner arching over to connect them.

You can also put a scarf on your penguin with other colors of tissue paper. Whatever your choice, you will end up with a shiveriffic penguin in 3d!

Activity #96: How Many Fish Can He Eat

Count with this penguin pal.

It's important for preschoolers to learn their numbers, but that doesn't mean you can't make it tons of fun to do so!

Cut out a large oval from black construction paper and a smaller one from white construction paper. Glue the white one on the middle of the black paper for the penguin's tummy. Glue on two white eyes with black dots in the middle and an orange beak.

Cut out orange feet and paste them on the back of the bottom of your black oval, so that you can see them from the front.

Finally, cut out two more oblong shapes from the black construction paper for the wings. Instead of gluing these on, though, pin them on with two brass tacks (the kind that you has two flaps that can be splayed out once you push them through the paper).

Now, gather together a bunch of edible goldfish to play a game with your new penguin. Set out a number of goldfish (say, three to start) on the white part of the penguin.

Ask your little one how many fish there are. Have them count, starting with one. If they get the answer right, move the penguin's wings up into a triumphant position and praise your child.

Allow him or her to eat the goldfish if it is snack time. Then, lay out a different number of fish. You can also play this same game with gummy fish. Enjoy!

Christmas

Activity #97: Advent Christmas Tree

Count down the days.

Anticipation can be such agony! To help your little one be patient about waiting for Christmas to come, have them create an advent tree to count the days until the holiday.

Cut out a large tree shape from green or blue construction paper (or use white and paint or color it green or blue). Decorate your tree with silver or gold ribbon and glitter.

Now, stack a bunch of colored papers together (five or six for thin paper, two or three for more construction paper) and cut out circles to act as tree ornaments. Also cut out a gold star. Write the numbers 1 to 25 on the ornaments.

To attach the ornaments, you have a couple options. If you want to glue down pieces of Velcro on the tree, with the opposite pieces on the ornaments, you can make this advent calendar be something you use every year. Have your child Velcro an ornament on the tree every day before Christmas, putting the star at the top on Christmas Day! Otherwise, you can have your child glue or tape the ornaments on the tree each day and make a new advent calendar next year.

Activity #98: Angelic Candle Holder

To light Santa's way!

Cut off the top of a Styrofoam cone so that you can fit the opening of a two-inch clay pot down over the cone snugly. If it doesn't fit quite right and is a little loose or wiggles, glue it in place with hot glue.

Stick a small piece of clay down into the pot (filling it about half way) and then put a tea light on top of it. You can use battery powered tea lights to be safer, or only light a real tea light when the angel is finished and put up high out of reach of little hands.

Now, you and your child need to make the angel.

Cut a circle out of your choice of colored construction paper for the face of the angel. Draw on eyes with pretty long eyelashes and a mouth. Glue on yarn for hair, making sure to cover the entire back and the sides of the face.

Now choose a pretty fabric for the dress (something gold or silver looks especially nice for an angel, but it can be anything). Wrap it around the rest of the cone and glue it on.

Finally, add a little sash as a pretty accessory, tying it into a bow at the back. The candle flame (whether real or battery powered) acts as the halo once it is lit.

You can make a number of these little angels which also make heartwarming Christmas gifts for others.

Activity #99: Custom Wrapping Paper

Nothing is more special.

Most wrapping paper just gets thrown away as soon as a gift is opened without the recipient even looking at it. Not anymore.

Have your child make his or her own wrapping paper that will be sure to be examined and cherished.

Using brown butcher paper that comes in a long roll on a tube, have your child decorate with stamps.

You can use the Christmas themed sponge stamps available at any craft store as they are big and super fun (as well as nice feeling in little hands).

Try to choose a couple different colors of paint/ink and space the stamp prints out as evenly as possible. Let the paint dry before you wrap any gifts in it, but know that once you do, this personalized paper will be a huge hit.

Activity #100: A Team of Sled Pullers

Clothespin reindeer!

You can use either clothespins with the springs in them or the clothes pegs that are taller to make some reindeer to help pull Santa's sleigh.

Take two clothespins and turn one upside down. Now glue the ends (that you would normally hold) one on top of the other so that two of the 'legs' represent the antlers while the other two are the reindeer legs.

Glue some small craft eyes right below the antlers and a brown bead for a nose (a red bead works for a Rudolph reindeer).

Make a whole team of these guys so that they can pull a ton of toys through the sky.

Activity #101: Stick Him on Display

A magnetic gingerbread man.

Making a Christmas magnet has never been easier now that they sell magnet strips at any craft store. You can make all sorts of magnets, but gingerbread men are especially cute and relevant for a kitchen!

Cut out a gingerbread man shape from brown construction paper or poster board (which will make it a little sturdier). Draw a face on the gingerbread man, as well as some buttons on his tummy.

Dab some glue all along the outline of him and have your little one shake glitter over the glue. Let it sit for a minute and then shake off the excess glitter.

Finally, hot glue a magnetic strip on the back.

Other than gingerbread men, you can follow the same steps to create other Christmas themed magnets. You can make trees, snowmen, angels, elves, penguins, or whatever you want. Not only do magnets dress up your kitchen fridge for the holidays, they also make great gift accessories for teachers, grandparents, or friends.

Activity #102: Expedition to the North Pole

A standing sign to point the right way.

To make this very simple decoration or table centerpiece, take a cardboard paper towel tube and cover it with white paper, gluing or taping it to secure.

Now, draw red stripes with two lines going around the pole at a diagonal angle and have your child color them in with red. There should now be alternating red and white stripes running down the pole.

Next, cut out an arrow shape from cardstock. Have your little one decorate it with glitter, leaving a space in the middle. Write North Pole in the middle of your arrow and glue it onto the tube, about a third of the way down from the top of the tube.

Now, take a rectangular block of Styrofoam and carefully push the bottom of the pole down into the block. Spread on some glue to the surface of the block and sprinkle some fake snowflakes (purchased at any craft store) onto the glue. You can also add some silvery glitter to make the snow shimmer.

Finally, wrap a red or green (or both) ribbon around the block of Styrofoam to make it more festive.

Set your new North Pole sign on the mantle, in the middle of the dinner table, or on the counter for a very unique and interesting decoration.

Activity #103: Hang 'Em High or Low

Elf heads for the tree.

Paint a Styrofoam ball the color you want for the elf's head. Push a lollipop stick into the top of the ball a little ways.

Now, wrap a piece of felt (red or green, or any color you want) into a cone so that the point comes together at the top of the lollipop stick. Glue the felt into place around the Styrofoam ball and at the top of the stick. Cut out a gold or silver band of ribbon to wrap around the bottom of the pointy elf hat. Add a pom pom or a silver bell to the point with hot glue.

Now draw a cute elf face on the front with eyes, a nose and mouth. Glue another length of ribbon around the bottom of the ball to act as a collar. You can either settle your new ornament into the tree between the branches, or add a string to the stop of the hat to hang it.

Enjoy your little elf, or make many of them to keep each other company amongst all of your other ornaments.

Bonus Activity: Perfect Poinsettia Wreath

Hang it up on your front door for holiday spirit.

Trace your child's hands many times on both red and green construction paper. Then, cut out the shapes and arrange them in a circle. You should have a ring of green hands on the outside (these will be the leaves of the poinsettia flower).

Then, make a ring of red leaves and another inside that until there is no hole in the middle of your wreath. Glue all of the hands together in this sequence.

In the very middle, you might want to add a small white paper circle. Put a few dabs of glue on the red hands in random places and sprinkle some red glitter on for a sparkly effect.

Last but not least, attach a ribbon to the back of the wreath in order to hang it on the front door.

CPSIA information can be obtained
at www.ICGtesting.com
Printed in the USA
LVHW022203301120
673086LV00059B/3130